Today I Saw A Ladybug

Crystal V. Carroll

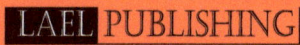
LAEL PUBLISHING

Today I Saw A Ladybug

by Crystal V. Carroll
Published by Lael Publishing, LLC
Winston Salem, North Carolina
www.LaelAgency.com

No part of this book may be used or reproduced in any form, stored in a retrieval system, or transmitted in any form by any means, electronic, photocopy, mechanical, recording or otherwise without written permission from the author. The only exception is for critical articles or reviews, in which brief excerpts may be used.

Paperback ISBN - 978-1-954433-03-8
Hardback ISBN - 978-1-954433-06-9

Author's Contact: CrystalsLadybugCreations@gmail.com

Copyright © 2021 by Crystal V. Carroll
All Rights Reserved

First Edition

Printed in the United States of America.

Dedication

This book is dedicated to my loving husband Ignatius "Iggy" and our inspirational children, Kennedy and Emerson. I love you to the moon and back.

To my steadfast family, thank you for always encouraging me to SHINE.

In loving memory of my dad, Clinton Jr., gone but never forgotten.

Today I saw a Ladybug!
I was feeling sad before.
I'd lost something I'd loved so much.
But Ladybug reminded me, my heart should not be sore.

She fluttered first around my head,
Her wings so red and bright!
And then she landed on my hand,
Taking rest from her long flight.

Sometimes my heart feels like her spots,
Dark in a world that's light.
But Ladybug reminded me
Sometimes that happens, and it's all right.

Like Ladybug, you are around
Even when I can't quite see.
I'm not really alone,
You're always here with me.

Like Ladybug, you've always loved
To simply say hello.
To visit me, and come to see,
The next stage of my life show.

I know you would be proud of me,
The growth I make each day.
Even if, like friend Ladybug,
There wasn't long to stay.

And just like that, the Ladybug is now taking her flight!
Good-bye dear friend, thank you, take care!

Until the next time that we meet, I'll move forward. See you there!

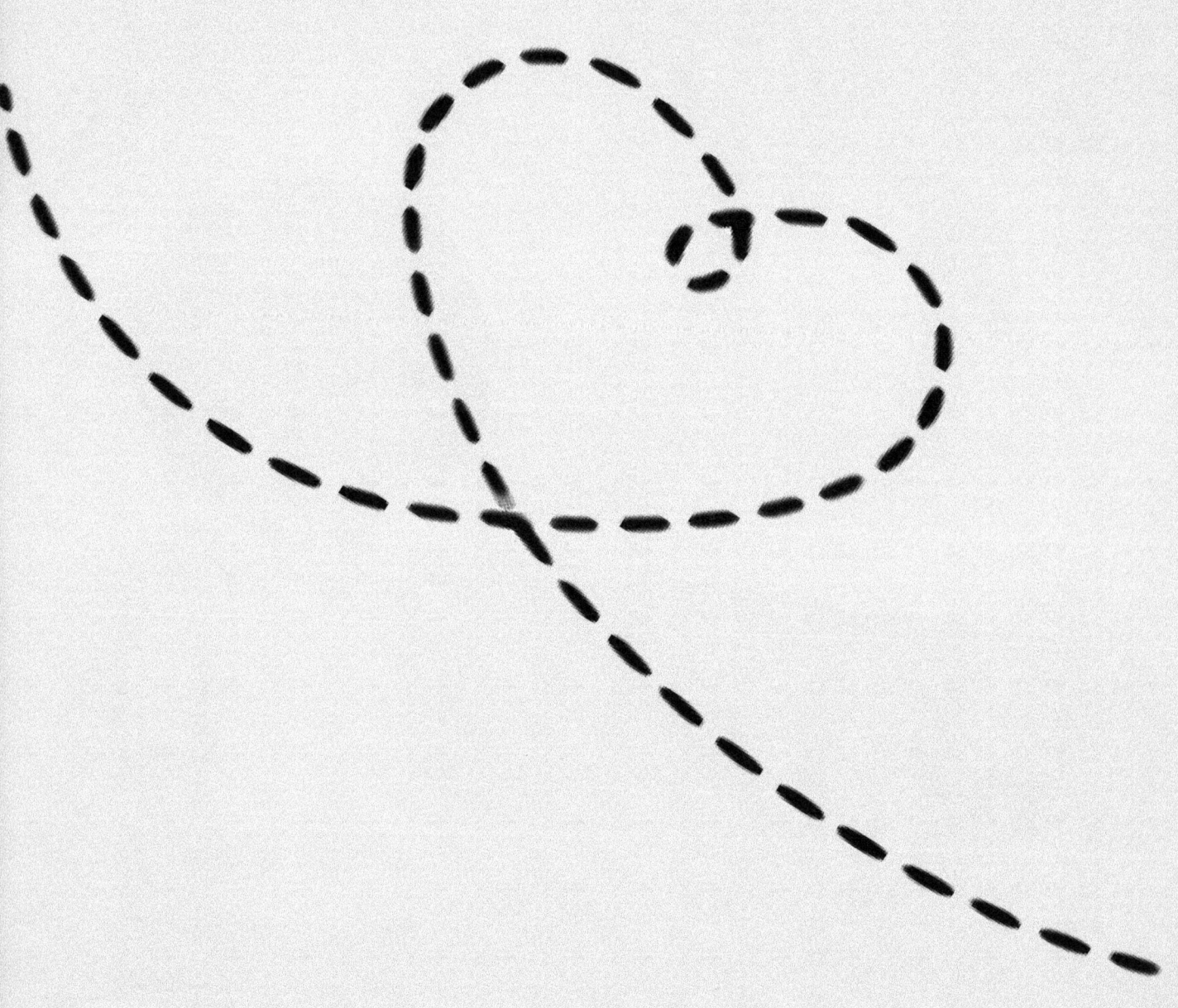

About the Author

Crystal V. Carroll is the CEO of Crystal's Ladybug Creations, LLC. A company she created to remind individuals of their self-worth and empower people of all ages to always SHINE! As the owner –wife, mother, daughter, sister, and friend – she is committed to helping others resist the negative experiences and societal feedback meant to dim our individual light. She believes that positivity and self-expression about the things that matter most, including a relationship with God, family connections, good health, community involvement, generational financial growth, to name a few, can help us to be whole and live our BEST LIFE.

Crystal resides in Miami, Florida. She is a devoted wife to a compassionate first responder and a very present mother of two amazing young adults.

www.ingramcontent.com/pod-product-compliance
Lightning Source LLC
Chambersburg PA
CBHW041229240426
43673CB00010B/284